THE ROCK-HOUND'S BOOK

The Rock-Hound's Book

SEYMOUR SIMON

Illustrated by Tony Chen

The Viking Press   New York

For Joyce, who collected by my side

contents

are you
a Rock Hound?

Have you ever bent down and picked up a rock from the ground? Almost everyone has. Did you like its color or did it have an interesting shape? Did it catch your eye because it glittered in the sunlight? Perhaps you put the rock in your pocket and brought it home. If you did, you were on your way to becoming a rock hound.

Rock hounds are people who enjoy finding and collecting rocks and minerals. They collect rocks for fun, just as others collect stamps or coins. But rock collecting can be more than just a hobby. It can be an adventure, a scientific study—even a business.

It's all up to you. You can collect rocks from just around your own neighborhood or make collecting

trips to near or distant places. You can trade or buy
and sell rocks from all over the world. You can join
rock-hound clubs and make many friends who are
interested in the same things you are.

Rock hounds learn how to identify rocks and minerals, and they discover why some kinds are found

only in certain places. They learn about the history of the earth and how the rocks were created. They learn which rocks are rare and valuable and which ones are commonplace and useful.

This book is for rock hounds who are just beginning. It will help you to identify what you find. It will tell you how to go about setting up your collection. But the book is not just for reading. It's an invitation for you to go out and explore the world of rocks and minerals.

minerals, rocks, and gems

Have you ever played the game "Animal, Vegetable, or Mineral?" In that game, one player thinks of an object and gives a clue so that the others can guess. To the players, a "mineral" is anything that isn't "animal" or "vegetable." But to a scientist, the word "mineral" has a much more special meaning.

A scientist may define a mineral as a substance formed from inorganic (nonliving) things found naturally in the earth. Not all scientists agree exactly with this definition. Some scientists think that a mineral must be solid and not liquid. Others call coal a mineral even though it formed long ago from living plants. Still other scientists say that a mineral is any natural substance that makes up a rock.

You can see that it's not so easy to tell what a mineral is in just a sentence or two. So let's explain the definition of a mineral and then add a bit to it. "Inorganic" or "nonliving" means that coal, wood, bones, seashells, and pearls (all of which come from living things) are not minerals. "Naturally found" means that a mineral cannot be made by humans. Even if a scientist makes an exact duplicate of a mineral in a laboratory, it is not considered a mineral since it is not naturally found.

Now that we've said what minerals aren't—what are they? Minerals, like everything else, are made of certain chemical substances called elements. The smallest part of an element is an atom of that element. Atoms are far too small to be seen even with the most powerful microscope, but scientists know that they exist. Scientists can weigh and measure atoms and find out how they combine with each other.

In the entire earth only ninety-two different elements are found in nature. Of the ninety-two natural elements, only about ten are commonly found in a pure state. These include gold, platinum, copper, sulfur, and carbon. These are all considered minerals. But there are about two thousand more minerals that have so far been found in the earth. All of these minerals are made up of two or more of the ninety-two natural elements.

When an element combines chemically with one
or more other elements, a "compound" is formed.
Most minerals are compounds rather than elements.
Iron pyrite (sometimes called fool's gold), for example, is made up of the two elements iron and sulfur.
The same two elements in different amounts form
a mineral called pyrrhotite. Unlike pyrite, pyrrhotite
is attracted to a magnet. These two minerals also
look different from each other. They may be colored
differently and have different shapes even though
they contain the same elements.

Many minerals are found in the form of beautiful
crystals. Crystals are regular shapes that are made
by the atoms of a mineral. Quartz crystals are different from crystals of pyrite, but all crystals of the
same mineral look alike. Pyrite crystals are always
cube shaped. In fact, you can often identify a mineral by the shape of its crystals. But don't expect
to always find large, perfectly shaped mineral crystals on your collecting trips. Most crystals are rather
small. Sometimes a magnifying glass will help you
to pick out tiny crystals in a mineral you find.

Some crystals, such as diamonds, emeralds, ru-
bies, and sapphires are called gems. Gems are minerals that are beautiful when cut and polished. Some
gems, such as diamonds and emeralds, are rare and
valuable. Many other gems, such as garnets, ame-
thysts, and opals, are beautiful but are not so rare.

They are sometimes called semiprecious gems. Most gems are very hard and do not scratch easily. This makes them suitable to be worn as jewelry.

It would take a long time to describe each of the approximately two thousand minerals known to scientists. Of all these minerals, only about thirty are called rock-forming minerals. They make up almost all of the rocks you are apt to find on the earth's surface. Some minerals are valuable for the metals they contain. Metal-bearing minerals are called ores. In this book, we'll concentrate on the more common rock-forming minerals.

Suppose you find a rock near your home that you know contains quartz because you recognize the crystal shape. You still do not have enough information to identify the rock because rocks are made of a mixture of minerals or other rocks. Rocks are hard, natural parts of the earth's crust.

Some rocks are mostly one mineral with small amounts of other minerals. Other rocks are mixtures of several different minerals. Certain kinds of rocks are even made from different kinds of rocks that have been naturally cemented together.

The minerals that make up rocks are usually found in the form of particles or grains. In different rocks, the grain may be large or small. Sometimes the grains are too small to be seen without a magnifying glass. The mineral grains of a rock may be scattered about or arranged in layers. The size and arrangement of the mineral grains help to identify the kind of rock.

Actually, there are thousands of different kinds of rocks. There are rocks of all colors: red, green, black, yellow, white, and blue. There are smooth rocks and rough rocks. There are shiny rocks and dull rocks. There are rocks made up almost entirely of one mineral, and rocks made up of many minerals.

Although rocks can be grouped in different ways— by the minerals they contain, by their appearance, by ways in which they are used by man—most of the time, they are grouped according to the way in which they were formed. According to this method of classification, the three main classes of rocks are *igneous, sedimentary,* and *metamorphic.*

Igneous rocks form by the cooling and hardening of hot, molten rock from within the earth. The word "igneous" means "having to do with fire." Examples of igneous rocks are granite, gabbro, and basalt.

Sedimentary rocks come from other rocks and minerals which were worn down or dissolved in ocean water. All rocks wear down under the forces of erosion: wind, running water, heat, and cold. Rock fragments called sediments roll downward from high places such as hills and are carried along by streams and rivers till they reach the oceans or low-lying places on land.

As more and more sediments are deposited over the years, the layers of loose material become hard and compact. Over long periods of time they turn into rocks. The kinds of sedimentary rocks the layers become depends upon the size, shape, and chemical nature of the particles. Examples of sedimentary rocks are sandstone, shale, and limestone.

Some rocks come neither from molten rock nor from sediments. Yet they resemble rocks in these groups. They are called *metamorphic rocks,* rocks that have changed their form. In some metamorphic rocks, new minerals formed under great heat and pressure, and the appearance of the rock changed greatly. Other metamorphic rocks are hardly changed at all. Examples of metamorphic rocks are slate, marble, and quartzite.

Think of igneous rocks as the first or parent rocks of the earth's crust. When igneous rocks weather they break into fragments which are deposited and form sedimentary rocks. These in turn may be changed into metamorphic rocks. Sometimes high temperatures beneath the earth remelt the rocks and form new igneous rocks to complete a "rock cycle."

where to look

You've already begun to collect if you've ever picked up a rock or stone and brought it home with you. Perhaps you found an especially pretty one on a beach, or perhaps a rock with little specks of a glittery mineral attracted you. Even a trip to a nearby vacant lot can start you collecting. Look for freshly broken rock or break a piece yourself. The fresh break will give you a much clearer clue to the rock's identity. A rock exposed to the air and the rain for long periods of time changes in color and general appearance.

Compare the rock you find with others in the general area. Are there similar rocks around? Do some kinds of rocks often show up together in the same places? Does a nearby park also have the same kinds of rocks? Why might you expect that to be the case?

Sometimes you may find a rock that is neither like the others around it nor like some nearby underlying rock, or bedrock. The rock may have come from an area many miles away. From the northern United States, many rocks were carried southward by glaciers during the Ice Ages. These rocks tell us the kinds of rocks the glaciers picked up on their trip south.

After you have collected rocks in your own neighborhood, there will come a time when you will want to collect farther afield. You will want to collect something new and different from the rocks you've come to know. But where's a good place to find new rocks?

Find out if there is a road cut or a building excavation that you can get to. Digging and blasting into bedrock is something that you can't do yourself. But there's no reason you can't pick up some of the scrap rocks left behind by such an operation. Again, look for freshly broken pieces of rock.

Another good place is a sand pit or gravel bank. Many different kinds of quartz can sometimes be found there. A clay bank sometimes turns up specimens of interesting minerals and maybe even fossils (see page 66). Digging in clay is hard, dirty work. So remember to dress in old clothing and take along a sturdy shovel.

The beds of streams, the bases of cliffs, and places where underlying rock comes to the surface are other spots to look. Remember that broken rocks roll downhill and are also carried downstream by running water. An eroded hillside sometimes reveals interesting finds.

If you live near a beach, you will find it worth

a rock-collecting visit. Many beaches have beautiful
rocks that are worn smooth by the constant tumbling
of water and sand. Wet rocks are very beautiful, but
when they dry, they may lose some of their sheen.
To make them regain their sparkle at home, try ap-
plying a thin coat of mineral oil.

Another good place to visit is a stone-cutting factory or a place that sells mason's materials. Ask for permission to pick up small chips of rocks and minerals. You may be able to collect bits of granite, marble, limestone, slate, and many other kinds of rocks.

But perhaps the most interesting place to collect is a quarry or a mine. You need not even go into the mine or quarry. Look instead at the surrounding piles of discarded waste rocks and minerals. These heaps, called dumps, are full of battered chunks of rocks and minerals. You can spend hours poking around in a dump and finding things to collect.

At the back of this book there is a list of books and magazines that have maps on which you can locate many mines and quarries. You can also obtain maps showing mineral deposits by writing to the United States Geological Survey, Washington, D.C. 20242. Also write to the department of mines or the geological survey of your home state. This is usually located in the state capital. Use a phone book or ask your librarian for the exact address.

The kinds of rocks and minerals that you find will depend on where you look. The deserts of the southwestern United States, for example, are rich in quartz crystals, petrified wood, agate, opal, geodes, and pieces of all kinds of lava rock. Dry lakes in these regions contain borax, halite, and other salt minerals. Sometimes you may find crystal groups in a flower-like pattern such as "desert rose."

Rock and mineral collectors in the midwestern states are likely to find sedimentary rocks and the minerals that appear along with them, although places like the Black Hills of South Dakota, the Ozarks, and Minnesota have igneous rocks with mineral crystals.

Both the west coast and the northeast coast of the United States are good places to find igneous and metamorphic rocks and the many different kinds of mineral crystals that go along with them. Even some sedimentary rocks can be found along the coasts.

It's up to you to find out the kinds of rocks and minerals you are most likely to find in your own area. Your state geology department can help you.

Some Good Rock-Hound Rules to Remember

1. Always ask for permission before you collect on private property. If the mine or quarry is abandoned, ask someone who lives nearby where to obtain permission.
2. Ask also about any possible hazards, such as sliding rocks or steep sides. Most places will require an adult to be with you. He or she may also have to sign a statement clearing the owner of any responsibility for accidents.

3. Don't meddle with tools, machinery, or domestic animals that you may find.

4. Leave gates as you found them, either open or closed.

5. Don't walk or drive across growing crops. Stay on the road.

6. Take only what you will use for yourself or for trading. Leave some for the next rock hound, just as those before you left some for you.

7. Be courteous and considerate of the rights of others. As much as possible, leave things as you found them.

how to start collecting

Before you go on a rock-collecting trip, it is a good idea to plan ahead for it. First of all, it's only sensible to wear old clothes and sturdy, comfortable shoes. Even in the summer, wear long pants or slacks and a shirt with long sleeves. This will offer better protection against the sharp edges of rocks and also against insect bites.

Don't take too much equipment with you. Rocks are heavy, and digging and hammering for them is hard work. The less extra weight you have to carry, even for short distances, the more you can collect.

There are a few things that you will want to have with you so that you can collect more easily. The first thing you'll need is a hammer. The best kinds have a hard steel head and a steel handle. Hammers made of cast iron break and scratch easily when hitting rock. While you don't actually need one to begin with, a geologist's hammer with a flat head on one side and a pick on the other is something to think about if you become a dedicated rock hound.

Next, take along a bag or a sack made of a strong material such as canvas. It will be easier to carry if it has a handle or a strap. Cardboard boxes are not too good because they are apt to come apart in your hands if they get wet.

Bring along some newspaper or some grocery bags in which to wrap your specimens. Each rock or mineral should be wrapped separately before you place it in the bag. If you just put the rocks in without wrapping, they will rub against each other and break or crumble.

Carry along a notebook with you on your collecting trip. Write down the number of the specimen (start with number 1), the kinds of rocks around it, where you found it, and the date. Mark the specimen itself with a marking pencil or by sticking on a number with adhesive tape. This will come in handy after your collection has grown and you want to remember where you found something.

Not as necessary as the above, but useful under certain conditions, is a cold steel chisel, the kind

that's used on metal. A 6-inch or 8-inch chisel is very helpful in prying crystals out of cracks in the rocks. Thinner chisels are easier to use in narrow cracks. A magnifying glass for looking at small crystals and a pocket knife for testing hardness may also come in handy.

Try to start your collecting at a place where rock has been recently broken, such as a road cut, a mine dump, or a building excavation. Remember to ask permission before collecting on private property. *Be particularly careful around loose material on a hillside. It's easy to slip and hurt yourself.*

Only collect what you are likely to use or to trade with another collector. Don't smash up crystals you cannot take out yourself. There will be other rock hounds coming after you. Be conservation-minded even with seemingly inexhaustible supplies of rocks.

Rocks and minerals that have been exposed to rain, wind, and extreme temperatures may change in color and appearance and become hard to identify. Often the surface of the rock discolors and becomes brown or yellow. Therefore, you should either look for a freshly broken piece or use your hammer to break apart a large piece that looks interesting. *Caution: When hammering, do not attempt to hold the rock with one hand. Shield your eyes from possible flying chips.* Place the piece you want to break solidly atop another large rock. Look for a crack in the piece and try to hit along that line. You can also use a cold steel chisel to split the rock in the same manner.

Is your piece of rock similar to the bedrock in the area? Compare it to a part of the outcrop. (Bedrock is the solid rock that makes up the earth beneath its covering of soil and loose rock. An outcrop is a place where bedrock is exposed at the surface.)

A good size for specimens for your collection is about 4-inches wide by 4-inches long and perhaps 2-inches thick. Smaller pieces may not show the properties of the rock as clearly. Larger pieces are too heavy to carry and also take up too much room in display and storage. Use your hammer to trim each specimen to the size you want. You may find that you spoil several pieces before you get the knack of splitting a rock exactly where you want it.

During your first few collecting trips try to collect a great variety of rocks and minerals. Look for differences in color, hardness, mineral-grain size, and texture or feel. What these properties mean will become clear when you identify the rock. Remember to label each specimen with a number before you wrap it up and put it in your collecting sack.

Chopping minerals out of a large rock or from an outcropping takes a little more patience and skill than just picking up loose specimens. You most often will find mineral crystals in cracks or hollows in the rock of an outcropping. Crystals shatter easily. You have to chip them out carefully from the surrounding rock. Try to leave a piece of the rock, called a matrix, to set off the crystal.

Crystals in particular need special care in wrapping and handling. Tear a newspaper into squares large enough to wrap your specimen. Place several sheets of the paper on the ground with the specimen a third of the way from the bottom. Fold the bottom over, then the two sides, then fold the top down and around.

Small crystals that you want to keep can be wrapped in paper or in cotton and placed in plastic boxes. Certain crystals, such as halite (rock salt), will dissolve in moisture. Keep them from getting wet or damp.

As soon as you bring your specimens home, you can begin the interesting job of identifying them and learning about their properties. After a while, you will be able to identify many rocks and minerals by their appearance alone and others by simple tests that you can make in the field.

how to identify the minerals

Identifying a mineral specimen is something like guessing a suspect in a mystery story. One clue may not be enough in the mystery story, but as the clues build up the identity of the criminal becomes clear. In much the same way, it may not be enough to know one property of a mineral (though sometimes it is), but as you find out more properties you can usually identify the specimen.

Color is the most obvious property of a mineral, but may not be too dependable as a clue. Just a trace of a chemical can change a mineral into a completely different color. For example, pure quartz is colorless and looks like glass. But you can find specimens of quartz that are violet, rose, smoky, milky, green, black, or banded with different colors, depending on which chemicals they contain.

In a well-known textbook for advanced mineralogists, the author describes eight different colors minerals may have and many different shades of each. Still, color can be a help in identifying some minerals. Blue or green are typical colors of minerals containing copper. Examples of these are green malachite and blue azurite. Sulfur is yellow, cinnabar (a mercury ore) is reddish, and calcite is usually white. Your best bet is to use color as your first clue but not as a positive identification.

Streak is a more definite clue than color. The surface color of a mineral may vary from one specimen to another, but when different specimens are "powdered," they always have the same color if they are the same mineral. To make a streak or to "powder" a mineral, use a streak plate. This is just a piece of unglazed porcelain such as the back of a bathroom tile. To make a streak, you run the mineral against the tile.

Often, the color of the streak is different from the color of the mineral. Iron pyrite looks yellowish like gold but leaves a black streak. Gold leaves a yellow streak. A dark or black mineral will sometimes leave a streak that is much lighter. Biotite mica, for example, looks black in masses but leaves a colorless streak.

Luster is another property easy to tell by looking. Luster is the way a mineral shines in the light. Some minerals shine like a piece of polished metal. They are said to have a "metallic luster." Examples of minerals with this kind of luster are pyrite, galena, and pure metals such as gold and silver.

Nonmetallic lusters have various names which attempt to describe their appearance. Here is a list of nonmetallic lusters with examples of each.

Luster	*Example*
Vitreous or glassy	quartz, apatite, beryl
Adamantine or sparkling	diamond, wulfenite, cinnabar
Pearly	talc, gypsum, calcite
Resinous or waxy	sphalerite, willemite, microlite
Silky	asbestos, malachite
Greasy	nepheline, herderite
Dull	chalk, clay, bauxite

Hardness is a property for which you have to test. Hardness does not mean how easily a mineral can break; rather, it is a measure of how easily it can be scratched. If you scratch a mineral against a substance of known hardness, the harder one will leave a scratch on the softer one.

The relative hardness of minerals was arranged in a scale many years ago by a German mineralogist named Friedrich Mohs. He numbered ten minerals from the softest, talc (1), to the hardest, diamond

(10). Here is Mohs's scale as it is still used today.

1	Talc	6	Feldspar
2	Gypsum	7	Quartz
3	Calcite	8	Topaz
4	Fluorite	9	Corundum
5	Apatite	10	Diamond

Any mineral on the scale will scratch any mineral with a lower number and will in turn be scratched by minerals with a higher number. You don't need a complete set of these minerals to test for hardness, however. The scale below isn't as accurate as Mohs's but will usually give you a good idea of an unknown mineral's hardness.

Your fingernail can scratch	1 and 2
Penny with pressure can scratch	3
A steel knife can easily scratch	4
A steel knife can barely scratch	5
A steel knife can be scratched by	6
Glass can be scratched by	7
Quartz can be scratched by	8

Cleavage and *fracture* describe the ways in which a mineral can break. Most minerals fracture in an irregular way instead of cleaving smoothly along a flat, even surface. Some minerals, such as quartz and tourmaline, show a rounded fracture called conchoidal. Conchoidal means shell-shaped. Glass and the rock obsidian also show conchoidal fracture.

Minerals can cleave in one direction or in several directions. Pieces of mica, for example, split easily

FRACTURE

CONCHOIDAL FRACTURE:
OBSIDIAN

UNEVEN FRACTURE:
ARENOPYRITE

EARTHY FRACTURE:
CLAY

CLEAVAGE

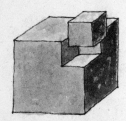
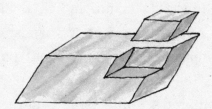
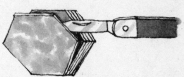

CUBIC CLEAVAGE:
GALENA

RHOMBOHEDRAL CLEAVAGE:
CALCITE

BASAL CLEAVAGE:
MICA

into flat sheets in only one direction. Feldspar splits in two directions that meet at nearly right angles. Galena (lead ore) and halite (rock salt) split in three directions and form cubes. Other forms of cleavage do not meet at right angles and may have more sides. This is a difficult property to judge, but remember that most minerals do not show cleavage in more than two directions.

Other properties may help in identifying one or another mineral. For example, some minerals, such

35

as magnetite, are attracted by a magnet. Others, such as willemite, will glow or fluoresce in different colors when exposed to an ultraviolet light (see page 65). Certain minerals have a definite taste, while others may have an odor.

Minerals also differ in their specific gravity or their weight compared to the weight of an equal volume of water. A piece of gold, for example, has a specific gravity of about 19. That means it is about 19 times heavier than an equal volume of water. The specific gravity of quartz is only about $1\frac{1}{2}$. A piece of quartz feels much lighter than the same-sized piece of gold. For your purposes, it is not necessary to measure this exactly. Hold a mineral in your hand and bounce it up and down. The heftier it feels compared to others the same size, the higher is its specific gravity.

There are still other ways in which minerals can be identified, such as by the shape of their crystal or by chemical tests. But the properties described above are enough to help you identify most common minerals. List your findings about an unknown mineral on an index card like the one shown opposite. Then turn to the lists at the back of this book and match the properties with one of the minerals listed. As you collect some of the more common minerals you will learn to identify them by recognizing two or three of their properties.

Mineral number _11_

Color *black* Streak *white* Luster *pearly* Hardness _2-3_

Breakage *thin flakes* Other properties noticed *mineral can be bent back and forth without breaking*

Can you tell the sample mineral?

minerals
all around you

There are about two thousand different kinds of minerals known. But only about twenty-five to thirty make up almost all of the rocks on the earth's surface. These are called the rock-forming minerals. Some are more common than others. Here are some of the minerals you are most likely to find on your next collecting trip.

Quartz is the most common mineral on earth. Beach sand is mostly finely ground quartz. Quartz is found in many kinds of rocks, including granite, schist, and gneiss. Quartz is also found in pure crystal form, frequently in cavities in rocks, and sometimes in a hollow rock ball called a geode. Sometimes quartz crystals are small and few in number.

Other times the crystals are very large and appear in masses. Quartz is not always so easy to recognize. It comes in a variety of colors, and its luster varies from glassy to waxy.

Quartz is an important mineral in industry. Quartz sand is used in making glass. Quartz crystal is used in electronics and for optical purposes. The colored varieties of quartz such as amethyst, agate, and rose quartz are considered semiprecious gems and are used in jewelry.

Identifying quartz. First try scratching the mineral with a knife. Quartz cannot be scratched even by a good steel knife. Quartz can be used to scratch glass. Quartz crystals are always six-sided and have a glassy luster. Broken quartz shows a conchoidal fracture. Crystalline quartz varieties include rock crystal, milky quartz, rose quartz, smoky quartz, amethyst, citrine, and several others.

Noncrystalline quartz can be identified by its hardness and by its waxy luster. Noncrystalline quartz varieties include jasper, agate, opal, flint, chert, carnelian, and chalcedony. Many of these have beautiful bands of different colors and are used for jewelry.

Feldspar is the name for a group of related minerals. All of the feldspars are similar but each has a slightly different chemical makeup. Quartz is more common than any single kind of feldspar, but taken together all the feldspars are five times more common than quartz. The feldspar group makes up about 60 percent of the earth's crust. Feldspars are part of most of the rocks that were formed from molten material.

Identifying feldspar. It's a good idea to first learn the properties that all feldspars have in common. Then later on you may want to learn how one feldspar mineral differs from another. All feldspars have a hardness of 6, just hard enough to scratch ordinary window glass. They have good cleavage in two planes which are at almost right angles to each other. Feldspar has about the same heft as quartz. Luster varies from glassy to pearly. Since feldspar weathers to become clay—and loses its luster in the process—check the luster at a fresh break.

It is easy to confuse feldspar with quartz. The best way to tell them apart is by feldspar's cleavage, nearly right-angled. Calcite also looks like feldspar but is much softer. The most common kinds of feldspar are orthoclase, microcline, plagioclase, albite, and oligoclase. Their colors are usually white, pink, or gray. Don't worry about telling them apart. Just try to identify them as feldspars.

Calcite is found in many varieties around the world. Next to quartz, calcite is the most abundant single mineral. It is the main mineral in limestone and marble, rocks used in building and sculpture.

When water drips from the ceilings of caves in limestone-rich areas, deposits of calcite form like icicles. The ones hanging from the cave's roof are called stalactites; the ones growing up from the floor are called stalagmites. Other kinds of calcite are named for the shape of the crystals they form, such as dog-tooth spar and nail-head spar. Iceland spar is a clear variety of calcite that was first found in Iceland.

Clear calcite such as Iceland spar has a fascinating optical quality. Place a piece of Iceland spar over a printed page. You'll see double. Calcite bends light in such a way that anything seen through the crystal appears to be clearly doubled.

Identifying calcite. Calcite can be scratched with a penny. In fact, you may be able to scratch it in some places with your fingernail. Calcite shows very good cleavage in three directions. These are never at right angles with each other. Sometimes when you hit a piece of calcite, it breaks into a six-sided solid called a rhomb.

Another way of identifying calcite is by a chemical test. Use a knife to scrape a small section of a piece of calcite into a powder. Put a drop of vinegar on the powder. Calcite reacts with a weak acid such as vinegar by bubbling rapidly.

White is the most common color of calcite. Pure calcite is white or colorless, but when it contains

Quartz

Gypsum

Asbestos

Apatite

Calcite

Malachite

Cinnabar

Sphalerite

Nepheline

Diamond

Willemite

Clay

Wulfenite

Microlite

Bauxite

Rose Quartz

Opal

Calcite

Amethyst

Microcline Feldspar

Muscovite

Smoky Quartz

Feldspar

Biotite

Agate

Labradorite

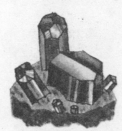

Hornblende

Carnelian

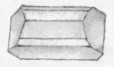

Feldspar

Garnet

small amounts of other chemicals it may be pale shades of pink, blue, green, yellow, or brown.

Mica is not a single mineral, but, like feldspar, is a group of related minerals. Mica is the mineral that most people recognize even if they are not rock hounds. Have you ever tried to peel sheets of mica? You can usually peel it into sheets thinner than the pages of this book.

Mica is found in rocks such as granite, gneiss, and mica schist. You can recognize it by the tiny flakes that glitter as you turn the rock in sunlight. Pure mica is used in the electrical industry as an insulator. Ground-up mica is used as insulating material, to plant seeds in, and as a lubricant. Mica flakes are used around Christmas time as the artificial snow you see in window displays.

Identifying mica. Even tiny bits of mica cleave into flat, smooth surfaces. Mica is quite soft and can be easily scratched with your fingernail. Micas usually have a pearly luster, but the color depends upon the variety. The most common forms of mica are muscovite, which is white; biotite, which is black; and phlogopite, which is brown.

Hornblende is another mineral found in many kinds of rocks along with mica. In fact, small crystals of hornblende in a rock are easily confused with small flakes of biotite mica. With a magnifying lens, you can see that mica has a wider, flat surface.

Hornblende is almost always dark green to black. Hornblende is most easily found as small dark crystals in a light-colored rock such as granite.

Identifying hornblende. Hornblende has a hardness of 5 to 6. It has a pearly or glassy luster. It cleaves easily but is often found in a fiber-like form. Hornblende is the most common mineral of a group called *amphiboles.* A mineral that looks much like hornblende is *augite.* It is found in most of the rocks which came from lava (igneous rock). Augite has about the same hardness, luster, and color as hornblende. The only difference between them is that they cleave at different angles, but this can only be seen with special equipment. Augite belongs to a group of minerals called pyroxenes.

Garnet is a gemstone as well as a rock-forming mineral. Like mica and feldspar, garnet is the name of a group of related minerals. One kind of garnet used for jewelry is pyrope, which has a deep blood-red color. It is sometimes called the Cape ruby.

Other kinds of garnet are often found in rocks such as schists. They may be dark red but are also yellow, green, or violet. The more common forms of garnet are ground up and used as abrasive for polishing. Red sandpaper is probably coated with crushed bits of garnet.

Identifying garnet. Garnets are very hard, from 7 to 7.5. Try using a garnet to scratch a piece of quartz.

Look at small garnet crystals with a magnifying lens. Large garnet crystals can be as big as baseballs. Most of the crystals you will find will be broken or fractured. They do not show cleavage. Garnets have a glassy luster. The most common kind of reddish garnet is almandite.

Minerals in your own area may include any or all of the ones mentioned in this chapter. But you may be living in a place where another mineral is even more common. Some places are rich in a mineral which may be scarce in most other areas. Perhaps there is a nearby rock-hound club you can contact for information about local minerals. Other sources that may offer you some assistance are the geology department of a local college, a state museum, or the department of education of your state. Also ask your librarian for periodicals or other information she may have on local minerals.

how to identify
the rocks

To identify a rock, it helps to know the kind and size of the mineral grains, their appearance, how the rock was formed, and where you found it. Remember that rocks are formed by different methods. The three different groups of rocks are igneous, sedimentary, and metamorphic.

IGNEOUS rocks, as described earlier, come from within the earth. A hot, molten substance called magma forms deep down. Often, a large mass of magma hardens before it reaches the surface. This kind of igneous rock is called intrusive. This means the magma "intruded" into other rocks. The rock cools slowly underground. Some intrusive rocks have single mineral crystals many feet long and several feet in diameter.

Magma that comes all the way to the surface and flows out of volcanoes or cracks is called lava. When lava hardens on the surface it is called extrusive igneous rock. The rate of cooling determines the size of the crystals or grains. Quickly cooling lava forms very small mineral grains. Some grains are difficult to see even with a magnifying lens. In some kinds of rock, such as obsidian, no mineral crystals form at all.

Granite is the most common intrusive igneous rock. When the mineral grains are very large, granite is called pegmatite. The rock is made of the light-colored minerals quartz and feldspar and a dark mineral such as mica or hornblende. The main color is from the feldspar and is usually pink or gray. You can easily see the glassy pieces of quartz and the cleavage planes of the feldspar. The dark minerals give granite a speckled appearance. Granite is found in mountain areas all over the world.

Beautiful, large mineral crystals often form in pockets in pegmatite. You may be fortunate to find gem minerals such as amethyst, quartz crystals, tourmaline, beryl, topaz, and garnet when you collect in a pegmatite area.

Diorite is a darker rock than granite. Its texture is much like granite but it is made up of about 75 percent feldspar, with the rest black mica and horn-blende. A few grains of quartz may also be present. Diorite is an intrusive rock and is often found along with granite. Diorite is found in the Adirondacks in New York State, in Massachusetts, and in much of Canada.

Gabbro is an even darker intrusive rock than diorite. It is made up of about 50 percent dark feldspar (plagioclase variety), with the rest augite, black mica, and olivine. Gabbro is dark green, dark gray, or black. It is common in the White Mountains of New Hampshire, the region around Lake Superior, and in many other mountain areas.

Peridotite is a dark intrusive rock with no quartz or feldspars. It is made up of dark minerals such as augite, olivine, and/or pyroxene. The most famous example is the peridotite mined in South Africa, in which diamonds are found.

Felsite is the name given to all extrusive rock that has a light color and a fine grain mineral. The grains are so fine that you can't recognize them even with a magnifying lens. Felsite contains the same minerals as granite, but the rock was formed by a surface flow of lava that cooled quickly. Felsites are found in volcanic or former volcanic regions.

Basalt is an extrusive rock with a fine grain that is black or very dark in color. It contains the same minerals as gabbro. Basalt is a heavy rock which is often crushed and used in railroad beds and underneath roads.

Obsidian is a black or very dark rock that looks like glass. It is often called volcanic glass. Because obsidian cooled so quickly, no mineral crystals formed at all. Obsidian is hard but brittle. It chips into thin, edged pieces and shows a shell-like fracture similar to glass. Because of its hardness, and the ease with which the edges could be made sharp, it was often used by the Indians of the West for making arrowheads and knives. Obsidian is found in many areas of the western United States but only rarely in the East.

Pumice is an extrusive rock that looks like a sponge with air holes in it. It was formed from lava while steam and other gases were still bubbling out of it. Pumice is a light rock, sometimes light enough to float on water. It is also a soft rock that you can scratch with your fingernail. Pumice is usually light gray.

Scoria is like pumice in appearance but its holes are larger. It is also harder and heavier than pumice. It is usually black or some dark color. Neither pumice nor scoria has crystal grains.

SEDIMENTARY rocks often appear in layers. You can see the layers in a cliff or when the side of a hill is cut through for a highway. The layers may be flat or bent and folded. A layer of sedimentary rock is usually different in color or texture from the layers above and below it. You can generally identify sedimentary rock by examining the bits of rocks and minerals that make it up. The size of the particles and how they were deposited determine what kind of rock was formed.

Conglomerate is made up of gravel and smooth, rounded pebbles. It is sometimes called pudding stone because it looks something like a pudding with nuts in it. The pebbles, usually quartz, are rounded from having been tossed around by waves or running water. Quartz conglomerate is a tough, sturdy rock. When the pebbles are sharp and pointed, the rock is called breccia.

Sandstone, as you can tell by its name, is made up of grains of sand cemented together. If you break off a piece with a hammer, you will be able to feel the grains of sand on the broken edge with your fingertips. Sandstone comes in all shades of yellow, red, brown, gray, and white. Sandstone is often used as a building rock and as a source of sand in making glass.

Shale is made from mud or clay. It is soft and easily broken. When shale is wet it has a strong earthy odor. Shale splits into very thin layers. Like clay, shale comes in many different colors. The most common colors are dark ones such as black, brown,

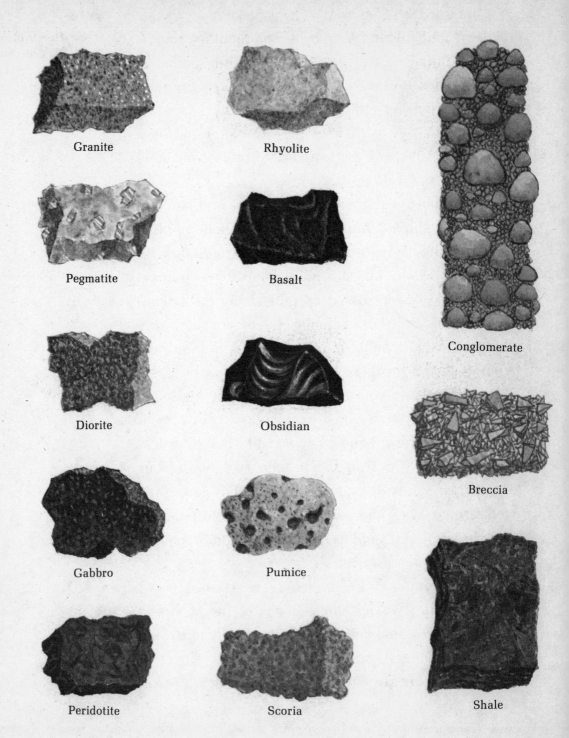

Granite

Rhyolite

Conglomerate

Pegmatite

Basalt

Diorite

Obsidian

Breccia

Gabbro

Pumice

Peridotite

Scoria

Shale

Sandstone

Marble

Hornblende Gneiss

Quartzite

Injection Gneiss

Limestone (shells)

Slate

Fossil Shell

Phyllite

Petrified Wood

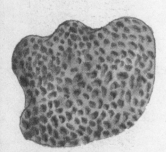

Tufa

Schist

Fern Fossil

and dark gray. Shale sometimes contains fossils, the hardened remains of plants or animals that lived in or around the muddy places in which the rock formed.

Limestone is formed from the action of water on the mineral calcite. Calcite dissolves in water and then is used by sea animals such as corals and clams to build their skeletons and shells. These animals die and over the years their bodies form a layer on the sea bed that becomes limestone. Sometimes you can find a shell or an impression of an animal in a piece of limestone. Blackboard chalk is a form of limestone. If you put a drop of vinegar on a piece of limestone it will bubble and fizz. Because water rapidly dissolves limestone, caves are often formed in limestone deposits. (See page 41.) Some of the best-known limestone caves are the Luray Caverns in Virginia, Carlsbad Caverns in New Mexico, and Mammoth Cave in Kentucky.

METAMORPHIC rocks are changed rocks. They are igneous or sedimentary rocks that have been altered by great heat, pressure, and chemicals. After the change they are completely different. Sometimes it is impossible to tell their original form. Even some of the minerals in them may have changed.

Marble is changed limestone. It is harder and heavier than limestone and may have crystals of calcite. Pure marble is white, but it may be colored red by iron oxides, green by serpentine, and black by carbon. Other marble colors are yellow, orange, and brown. Marble takes a beautiful polish and is used as an ornamental building stone. Marble scrapings react to acid (vinegar) as does limestone. Marble quarries are found in Vermont, Georgia, Tennessee, and Colorado.

Quartzite is a changed quartz sandstone. It is a heavy, tough rock in which all the empty spaces in the sandstone have been filled with crystals of quartz. The crystals of quartz glitter, giving quartzite a glassy appearance. Quartzite is the same color as the original sandstone—white, gray, red, or brown. A piece of quartzite breaks across the quartz grains rather than around them, as with sandstone.

Slate is changed shale. Slate is much harder and smoother than shale, but it splits into sheets in the same way. Thin slabs of slate are used for roof tiles and for chalk tablets. Slate may be black, gray, green, red, or purple. With a magnifying lens you can sometimes see small flakes of mica at the ends of a piece of slate.

Schist is also changed shale, but different kinds are formed from other rocks such as basalt or slate. The type of schist is named after its most abundant mineral. Mica schist is a common kind of schist that contains flakes of mica. Garnets are often found in mica schist. Other kinds of schist are talc schist, hornblende schist, and quartz schist. All schists are flaky rocks and appear in layers.

Gneiss is a changed rock made from many different rocks. It usually has large crystals and a banded appearance. Gneiss, like schist, is named after its most abundant mineral or rock. Gneiss usually has mica or hornblende arranged in alternate bands and this is a good way to identify it.

setting up
your collection

There's a difference between having a bunch of rocks in a drawer or a closet and having a rock collection. In a rock collection each specimen is identified and labeled. A collection is organized according to some general plan. It's probably more fun to have even a few rocks and minerals in an organized collection than to have a whole pile of unassorted and disarranged stones. There's no question about which way you will learn more.

Try to study the rocks and minerals as soon as possible after you've brought them home. Except for a few minerals such as halite (rock salt), wash each one carefully in some soapy water. Rub off loose material with a stiff brush. Be sure each specimen

shows a freshly broken side for easier identification.

Wait till they dry and then try to identify each one. Most of the minerals and rocks you find will be listed on pages 71–73. For unusual specimens refer to one of the guidebooks listed on pages 74–75. Try to learn how to identify each specimen so that you will be able to recognize it the next time you see it.

Label each specimen with a number written in ink on a small piece of adhesive tape. Put the same number on a 3 x 5 file card and write down the information you found out about it (see page 37). If you like, you can cross-index your collection by making out another card for each rock or mineral. On this card write the name first and then the number. Keep these in alphabetical order so that you can look up all the specimens of a particular mineral or rock you have in your collection. Keep your file cards carefully. They have all the information about your collection.

Setting up your rocks and minerals for display or storage is your next job. You can store most rocks and minerals in cigar boxes. Use heavy cardboard to separate each box into appropriate-sized squares. Try using a cardboard egg carton for smaller specimens. You can also make your own cardboard trays by folding and pasting. Painting or shellacking the containers will make them more attractive.

Small crystals and delicate specimens need more care. You can keep them on cotton in small plastic boxes. That's also a good way to display them. Minerals that flake easily, such as mica, can be sprayed with a clear plastic acrylic that you can purchase in any hardware store.

You'll probably want to keep on display some of your better-looking rocks and minerals. These should be neatly trimmed and cleaned. Remember that it is a good idea to leave some of the rock matrix in which a crystal is embedded. Prepare a neatly printed label for each item displayed.

Most specimens look better if they are placed on some kind of small pedestal. A clear plastic cube or a plastic box is just right. Paste the label underneath. Larger specimens can be mounted on blocks of wood that you can cut for the purpose. Paint the wood so that it looks more attractive. You can also use neatly cut pieces of styrofoam for this purpose.

Many hobby stores sell special metal mounts for displaying rocks and minerals. These are usually expensive, but look at them to get ideas about making similar mounts for yourself.

After you've collected a large number of rocks and minerals you may decide to set up a special kind of display. You may want to set up a display showing all the different varieties of quartz you've found. Or perhaps you will want to display minerals that show different colors or shapes. Displays of crystals, gems, or rock-forming minerals are still other ideas.

For your neighbors and friends, you may want to set up a display of the rocks and minerals common to your local area. This kind of display could also be exhibited in your school. Ask your teacher about it.

Visit museums that have rock and mineral collections and stores that sell rocks and minerals. Look for new ideas about how to display your own specimens at home. The chances are that you can find as many ways as you want to display your collection.

more ideas
for Rock Hounds

Besides collecting, there are many other things you can do if you are interested in rocks and minerals. Here are some ideas to get you started.

Join a rock-hound club so that you can meet with others who have the same interests. Rock-hound clubs are fine places for getting information about nearby collecting areas. Some clubs have trading sessions, talks about rock topics, outings, and other activities. Many clubs accept young members or have a junior division for people your age.

If you can't find the name of a local club from your science teacher in school or a librarian, consult the April issue of the magazine *Lapidary Journal*.

The issue lists close to fifteen hundred gem and mineral clubs around the world. Every state in the United States as well as many foreign countries have clubs listed. There's probably a club near you. Write to the address and ask for information about joining.

The sea and the sand take many years to polish the rounded pebbles you find on a beach. You can polish hard rocks and minerals to a shining smoothness in a much shorter time. To do this, you need a tumbler. Tumblers are just what you would expect: they are machines that use an electric motor to tumble rocks over and over again in a small rubber or plastic container.

Along with the tumbling rocks, you use a small amount of hard, grainy material called carborundum. This wears the surface of the rocks smooth. After you set the machine up, you let it run by itself for several days to a week. Then you replace the carborundum with a finer grain. The third week you use a still finer grain. The last week you use a fine polishing material.

Tumbling produces beautiful gemlike rocks and minerals. You can use them just for display, or you can easily make them into jewelry. Many hobby shops and rock and mineral houses sell blank mountings for rings, bracelets, tie clasps, cuff links, earrings, and pendants. A little dab of epoxy glue holds the polished rock or mineral in place in the setting.

Tumblers can be purchased from hobby stores and many department stores as well as from rock and mineral houses. The least expensive tumblers cost about ten dollars. Many stores also sell inexpensive tumbling material such as agate and obsidian, but you can use many kinds of your own rocks. The tumblers usually come with complete instructions and a variety of carborundum grits.

You can make crystals at home to see how they form different shapes, just as mineral crystals form different shapes in the earth's crust. Mix several tablespoonful of table salt with an equal amount of water. Add about a tablespoonful of ammonia water. *Caution: Do this in a well-ventilated place and be careful of splashing.* Place several pieces of brick or a few charcoal briquettes in a shallow pan. Pour the mixture over the brick or charcoal. Place a few drips of different-colored inks, food coloring, or other coloring matter on the mixture.

Leave the pan in a place where it will be undisturbed. In a few days crystals will start to grow over the surface of the bricks. They will be colored in the places you dropped some ink and colorless in the other places. This is similar to the way in which some mineral crystals became colored when they

form in the presence of small amounts of other chemicals.

Certain minerals are dull and uninteresting-looking in sunlight. But if you put some of them, such as willemite or autunite, in a dark room and use a special kind of lamp that gives off ultraviolet light, the ultraviolet rays will make these minerals glow in brilliant reds, greens, or yellows. The glow of a mineral under ultraviolet light is called fluorescence.

Many fluorescent minerals glow because of a small amount of another chemical in them. The calcite that comes from Franklin, New Jersey, glows bright red because of a small amount of manganese in it. The mineral dumps of the Franklin mines are well known for large amounts of different fluorescent minerals.

Ultraviolet rays are present in sunlight. They are the rays that darken your skin when you spend a day at the beach. But ultraviolet rays can be dangerous, particularly to your eyes. *Never look directly into an ultraviolet lamp.*

There are several different kinds of ultraviolet lamps sold for fluorescence. The best kind is known as a short-wave ultraviolet lamp. But that is also the most expensive kind. Ask if there is such a lamp in school that you may use. Perhaps a rock and mineral club that you join will have a lamp for use by its members. There are less expensive lamps that you can purchase. Check the list of supply houses on page 74 or a nearby hobby store.

Some rock hounds collect fossils as a sideline to their hobby. Fossils are the remains of animals or plants that have been preserved in rock for over ten thousand years. In the past, animals and plants were buried in the sediments of a sea, lake, or swamp.

The sediments piled up, and over the years turned to rock. So most fossils are found in sedimentary rock, rather than in igneous or metamorphic rock.

First find a likely fossil-collecting spot in an outcrop of sedimentary rock. The best places to look are where other fossils have been discovered in the past. You can find this information from some of the books listed on pages 74–75, by writing to your state geological survey, or by asking members of a nearby rock-hound club. In addition to your other rock-collecting gear, bring along a flat cold steel chisel and a magnifying lens.

When you get to the sedimentary rock outcrop, sit down. You need patience and time to find fossils. Running around from one spot to another is most often useless. Turn any loose rocks over carefully. Examine all sides with your magnifying lens. Many fossils are small and hard to see. You may be surprised to find how many rocks that you would ordinarily pass over have fossils in them.

With a chisel and a hammer, split rocks parallel to the layers. Most fossils are found on the flat surfaces between layers of sedimentary rocks. Don't try to remove any fossils from the rock because they break easily. Instead, chip the rock down to a small size that encloses the fossil. Number the fossil just as you would a mineral specimen. Wrap it in paper and bring it home.

At home, place the fossil rock in a container of water and let it sit overnight. Next day, use a stiff brush to remove any loose particles. You don't have to remove the fossil, but if you would like to try, use tweezers or a pocket knife blade to pry it loose. Try to identify the fossil and learn all you can about it. Write out your information on an index card numbered the same as the fossil. Read about how fossils are formed and visit a museum to see more fossils as your own collection grows.

Some minerals give off light if you crush them or scratch them. You can see this by scratching a metal file across a piece of sphalerite or corundum in a dark room. This is called triboluminescence.

Still other minerals will give off light if you heat them. Take a piece of fluorite and break it up into smaller bits. Put the bits in a baking dish with a glass cover. In a dark room, heat the dish over a low flame. The inside of the dish will look like a miniature fireworks celebration. Some pieces of calcite will also show this property. It is called thermoluminescence.

You can be a rock hound for just a short time or for all of your life. If your interest in rocks and minerals grows, you may take collecting trips far from home. If you are not able to travel to distant places yourself, you can still trade specimens that you collect nearby for others from all over the world. Even a common rock that you pick up outside your door may have formed within the earth millions and millions of years ago. Each rock is a bit of earth's history—past and present. And you, as a rock hound, are an explorer in time as well as space.

MINERAL CHECK LIST

To identify a mineral, first check the hardness and go to that group. Then check the other properties to see which fits. Most of the minerals you find will probably be on this list. If no description on this list fits a mineral you have, use one of the rock and mineral field guides listed on pages 74–75. The minerals in this group have a hardness of less than $2\frac{1}{2}$.

Mineral	Color	Streak	Luster	Hardness	Other Properties
Graphite	steel gray	gray	metallic	1	crystals rare
Talc	colorless, others	white	greasy	1	crystals rare
Gypsum	colorless, white, others	white	pearly	2	long, flaky crystals
Muscovite (mica)	colorless	white	pearly	2–$2\frac{1}{2}$	flakes easily
Halite	colorless	white	vitreous	$2\frac{1}{2}$	salty taste

The minerals in this group have a hardness of more than $2\frac{1}{2}$ but less than $5\frac{1}{2}$.

Mineral	Color	Streak	Luster	Hardness	Other Properties
Biotite (mica)	dark gray	white	pearly	$2\frac{1}{2}$–3	flakes easily
Galena	gray	gray-black	metallic	$2\frac{1}{2}$–3	crystal cubes
Calcite	colorless, white, pale colors	white	vitreous	3	crystals common
Barite	colorless	white	vitreous	3–$3\frac{1}{2}$	crystals common
Serpentine	green, white, others	white	dull	3–4	uneven fracture
Malachite	green	bright green	silky	$3\frac{1}{2}$–4	conchoidal fracture
Sphalerite	brown, black, others	light yellow to brown	adamantine	$3\frac{1}{2}$–4	crystals common
Fluorite	colorless	white	vitreous	4	crystals cube
Apatite	colorless, others	white	vitreous	5	conchoidal fracture
Limonite	brown	yellowish-brown	dull	5–$5\frac{1}{2}$	splintery fracture

The minerals in this group have a hardness of more than $5\frac{1}{2}$ but not more than 7.

Mineral	Color	Streak	Luster	Hardness	Other Properties
Magnetite	black	black	dull	$5\frac{1}{2}$–6	magnetic
Augite	black to green	gray-green	vitreous	$5\frac{1}{2}$–6	crystals and grains
Hornblende	green-black to green	gray-green	vitreous	$5\frac{1}{2}$–$6\frac{1}{2}$	splintery, crystal not common
Pyrite	gold-yellow	black	metallic	6–$6\frac{1}{2}$	"fool's gold"—looks like gold
Feldspar Group	white, many others	white	vitreous	6–$6\frac{1}{2}$	prismlike crystals
Hematite	black, dark colors	red	dull	$6\frac{1}{2}$	no crystals
Quartz	colorless, all colors	white	vitreous	7	crystals common, conchoidal fracture

The minerals in this group have a hardness of more than 7.

Mineral	Color	Streak	Luster	Hardness	Other Properties
Garnet	All colors, mainly brownish-red	white	vitreous	$6\frac{1}{2}$–$7\frac{1}{2}$	crystals very common
Tourmaline	black, others	white	vitreous	7–$7\frac{1}{2}$	found in igneous rock
Beryl	green	white	vitreous	$7\frac{1}{2}$–8	crystals found in pegmatite
Spinel	red, blue, green, other	white	vitreous	8	crystals, grains
Corundum	gray	white	vitreous	9	crystals common

WHERE TO BUY MATERIALS

The places listed sell rocks and minerals as well as rock-hound supplies of various kinds. The April issue of *Lapidary Journal* has advertisements for many other stores that sell rock-hound supplies. Local hobby and department stores sometimes have similar materials.

Aspen Lapidary, 6815 E. 48th Avenue, P.O. Box 1558, Denver, Colorado 80201 (catalog available).

Astro Minerals, 115 East 34th Street, New York, New York 10016.

Goodnow Gems U.S.A., 3608 Sunlite, Amarillo, Texas 79109 (price list of gems and minerals available).

International Import Co., 2420 Fawn Ridge Drive, Stone Mountain, Georgia 30083 (gem catalog available).

Lortone, Inc., 2854 N.W. Market Street, Seattle, Washington 98107 (catalog of tumblers and other equipment).

Murray American Corp., 15 Commerce Street, Chatham, New Jersey 07928 (price list of minerals available).

Star Diamond Industries, Inc., 1421 West 240th Street, Harbor City, California 90710 (catalog; also ask for free copy of *Gem Making as a Hobby*).

The Treasure Chest, Rt. 40 Box 54, Havre De Grace, Maryland 21078 (price list of minerals).

FURTHER READING

BOEGEL, HELLMUTH, *The Studio Handbook of Minerals*. New York: The Viking Press, 1971. (A)

CLAYTON, KEITH, *The Crust of the Earth*. New York: Natural History Press, 1967. (A)

GOLDEN NATURE GUIDE, *Fossils.* New York: Golden Press, 1962. (I)

GOLDEN NATURE GUIDE, *Rocks and Minerals.* New York: Golden Press, 1957. (I)

MACFALL, RUSSELL, *Gem Hunter's Guide.* New York: Thomas Y. Crowell Co., 1963. (C)

POUGH, FREDERICK H., *A Field Guide to Rocks and Minerals.* Boston: Houghton Mifflin Company, several editions. (A)

RANSOM, JAY ELLIS, *Fossils in America.* New York: Harper & Row, 1964. (A)

RANSOM, JAY ELLIS, *The Rock-hunter's Range Guide.* New York: Harper & Bros., 1962. (C)

SIMON, SEYMOUR, *The Look-It-Up Book of the Earth.* New York: Random House, 1968. (I)

SINKANKAS, JOHN, *Gemstones of North America.* Princeton: D. Van Nostrand, 1959. (C)

WYCKOFF, JEROME, *The Story of Geology.* New York: Golden Press, 1960. (I)

(A) Advanced books
(I) Intermediate books
(C) Books listing collecting areas

MAGAZINES

Gems and Minerals, P.O. Box 808, Mentone, California 92359.

Lapidary Journal, P.O. Box 2369, San Diego, California 92112 (April issue each year is the rock-hound buyer's guide).

Miami Gemcrafter, P.O. Box 616, Miami, Florida 33142.

Rocks and Minerals, Box 29, Peekskill, New York 10566.

Rocks and Minerals in Canada, Box 550 Campbellford, Ontario, Canada.

INDEX

Index